THE
FORGOTTEN
PEOPLE

DARRELL MILLS

PALMETTO
P U B L I S H I N G
Charleston, SC
www.PalmettoPublishing.com

Hardcover ISBN: 9798822962262
Paperback ISBN: 9798822962279
eBook ISBN: 9798822962286

AUTHOR'S NOTE

There's something incredible about letting a story unfold exactly as it comes to you. I never thought I'd be sitting here, writing these words, but God has a way of leading us to do things we didn't think we could. This book is no different—it's a piece of my heart, told the best way I know how.

You might notice a mistake here or there. It's not that I didn't try hard enough; it's that I wanted this story to stay raw and genuine, just as it flowed through me. My hope is that in its simplicity, it touches someone's heart, showing that our experiences—messy, unpolished, and real—are exactly what makes us who we are.

Thank you for letting me share this with you. May you find hope, healing, and perhaps even a little bit of yourself in these pages. God bless.

CONTENTS

THE FORGOTTEN PEOPLE

On a beautiful autumn day, something wonderful happened. A child was born around 10:15 a.m. Then suddenly things changed, and the child was pronounced dead. He was rushed immediately into a tub of cool water and was resuscitated. One could only imagine what the mother was going through when he was taken from her, on top of being alone in New York City in the 1960s.

What started as a family visit ended up being a life-changing event. He was three pounds and two ounces. He was born prematurely, three months early to be exact. As time went on, he was taken home. After six months, his mother noticed that he could not sit up. She began to take him to different hospitals—Johns Hopkins and Sinai Hospital were the two main ones they would visit. Through all the visits, they could not diagnose the problem.

As the medical bills started piling up, she began to get frustrated that she could not get medical coverage. While sitting in the foyer, she began to break down. That is when a stranger tried to console her. She began to tell the lady her dilemma, and the lady told her to take him to Kernan hospital. At Kernan's, they were able to determine that he had cerebral palsy.

Cerebral palsy is a neurological brain disorder that occurs during birth. In my case there was a lack of oxygen to the brain, which caused paralysis in my extremities—my legs and my left arm—and affected my vision and the curvature of my spine. After having three major surgeries, I have been told that I have a mild case of cerebral palsy. Every time that I hear that, I say to myself, "Really, if they only knew."

As a child, I quickly learned what I could and could not do. Also, having brothers, they took no pity on me. They "made me tough." They never said that I could be all that I wanted to be; they just wanted me to be strong and show no fear.

I remember sitting by the window and watching the other kids in the neighborhood running up and down the street playing, wishing that I could do the same. My mother said, "Go sit on the ledge where I can see you." When she said that, she stepped away, just for a minute, and when she returned, I was gone. She asked herself where I was, and she noticed that I was running with the other kids. I took off due to sheer excitement and have never looked back.

Before then I was always by myself. I was thinking about sports and music, trying to mimic every song I heard or every commercial I saw. That feeling is where I am most comfortable, even to this day. I remember a lady by the name of Miss Williams. Every time she saw me, she would say, "It's going to be all right, baby." She was about eighty years old, and I feel she may have seen a glimpse of my future.

I was just trying to be a kid. As time moved on, I found myself trying to fit into two different worlds: one where everybody around me was normal, and one where, years later, everybody was disabled. In the second one, people had helmets, wheelchairs, walkers, and the whole nine yards. All that I could say to myself was, "Wild, you're not alone in this." From there I began to interact with my peers. That is when I realized that they were dealing with similar things. Around then, I started to meet people from all over the city and surrounding counties. This made me look at people differently. We were all trying to fit in (which can be challenging because we are all constantly adjusting to what we are faced with).

Starting school at nine years old, I did not realize until I got older that I was already behind. I have no memory of preschool at all, but I do remember being in the hospital most of the time. It seemed like every summer, from a young age, I was in a full-body cast that was too tight the majority of the time. I pray that families prepare their children for the real world and watch out for the gift that God has placed in them. I also pray that, upon finding this gift, they help them to develop it instead of sheltering them if society would tend to feel sorry for them—that is not the mentality they need to operate with. It is true when they say only the strong survive, so do not tell them they are like everybody else because that is not true—they are different.

At a young age, children will stare, make fun of you, bully you, and mock the way that you are right in front of you. Try to imagine dealing with that while being back and forth to and from the hospital to have three major surgeries as a child. That is a lot to deal with, and support is crucial. I remember seeing Wes Unseld of the Baltimore Bullets and Johnny Unitas of the Baltimore Colts taking physical therapy while I was in the hospital. They were in the same room as me, and I was as star struck as a kid could be.

I should have never left William S. Baer School for two reasons: first, I was getting the individual instruction that I needed at the time, and second, I was not ready for public schooling. The psychological adjustment that comes with dealing with people who are not like you made me feel, at times, that I was living in two worlds. The only reason I left was because the guys who were my classmates were leaving one by one, so I followed. This was my first mistake. I came to realize that in life you are going to make a lot of mistakes, and that is ok. It is about how you recover, which is the most important thing.

For the most part, I enjoyed elementary school. It was not until middle school that things started to change. People started making fun of me, calling me names like Crip. Some would even want to fight me, but I was up for the challenge. I had two choices: to fight or to deal with my brother later when he would knock me up against the wall for not fighting back. I found out that my brother put the word on the street that anybody who touched me would have to deal with him. After he addressed it, it went from "show some respect" to "what's up, shorty," but the respite did not last long. That is when I realized that every family has one gangster. In my family, this, at the time, was very much needed. God was always watching if there was a call on your life.

There was a lady by the name of Mrs. Evans who invited all the kids in the neighborhood for ice cream and cake in her home. First, she took all of us into her basement and began to talk to us about the Bible. It was how she did it that got my attention. She seemed real with her presentation of the stories in the Bible, and she said that she was going to have Bible study every Saturday at 4:00 p.m. I started going every week, and I began to enjoy it. I was not going to miss a class.

After a few weeks, she made an announcement. After that class, she was going to give a Bible to the most outstanding student. What she said next came to pass. She said that in the coming weeks, the class was going to get smaller. With just being a kid, I did not know what that meant until later in my life. At the time all I knew was that I wanted to know more about this Jesus Christ. Rain, snow, any kind of weather, it did not matter to me. I could not wait for Saturdays. I was so eager to learn more, I did not miss a Saturday.

One day I looked around, and the class had begun to get smaller. The class went from twenty to ten to five to one within a matter of weeks. The prophecy was coming to fruition just like she'd said. It is amazing how God's gifts come to the forefront, and you do not even realize it until you get older and mature in the Lord later in life. So the day finally came, and when it was time for the presentation, all the kids came back to see who was going to win. After the class was over, she said, "I have one Bible to give out today for the most outstanding student—Darrell."

I took that children's Bible and began to look at all the pictures. I was curious as to why Jonah was in the mouth of a whale and why Daniel was put into the lion's den. That was the beginning of a lifelong journey that I am still trying to walk out. Please remember that I was still a kid with no formal biblical training, but what I did have was childlike faith and a hunger to know more about Christ.

I began to go to Mrs. Evans's house on Sunday morning for church, where her husband taught me a song that I sing to this day. I love that family, and if I happened to see them now, I would probably break down right in front of them. That family means so much to me. The last time I saw them was December 23, 1972. After the Sunday service was over, Mrs. Evans asked me about the plan of salvation. Of course, I did not know what she meant, but I could tell that it was something serious by the look in her eyes. By this point she had turned her chair to face me as she began to explain something that I'd never heard before. She asked me if I knew where I was going after I died.

As the silence hovered over the room, she began to explain what Romans 10:9 meant. She made it sound so simple, and by this time, I believed anything that she said. It is truly a blessing how the Lord used Mrs. Evans's family to make sure that I would spend eternity with the Savior just by confessing that I am a sinner. They came into my life to save me, and that is why I believe that Jesus died and rose again. I now sit at the right hand of the Father—it is that easy.

What they do not tell you is that walking it out is the hard part. As time went on, I was still trying to fit in. Having no prayer life and no mentor, with my oldest brother incarcerated and my other brother in another state, I was used to being alone. I say that to say this: if you are not grounded in the word, you will eventually fall off. That is exactly what happened to me.

I went back to doing what I thought was normal: watching sports and singing. I knew something had to change in my life, but I did not know who to talk to about it. If you do not talk to someone about it, you just keep it moving, because who is going to believe you if you say that at night you are having nightmares and you see shadows? I hated the nights. The mornings could not come fast enough, and this went on for years. God was still in control, even though I could not see it and was still trying to be normal.

Peer pressure is enormous. I saw that everybody around me had a girlfriend but I did not, so I asked myself why I did not, especially when the girls were drawing sticks to see who got the short one and she was the one who was going to be with me for the day. Going down memory lane, I now say that was their loss. People can be so cruel. You cannot let that control your destiny. I lived it and saw it—people taking things from you just because they could. Today they call that bullying. Trust me when I say that you can get through it; just say to yourself, "If God did not want me here, I would not be here." You have a purpose, no matter what life throws your way.

Back in the day, in junior high, there were so many people. The first year, I did great; but toward the end of the second year, the boys and I began drinking Wild Irish Rose, which made me laugh. They were drinking every day—whiskey and Colt 45—and smoking weed. By that time, I had a chip on my shoulder. I just did not care anymore and felt I needed to be heard at any cost.

When I was growing up, with authority figures, it was "do as I say," and that was the end of it, period. My parents did not recognize that I had a hidden talent. This talent was why I asked for record albums every Christmas. I love to hear other people sing, so I did not say anything at all about which records were chosen for me. With nothing else to do, I fell into the music daily.

All that my parents wanted for me was to be protected by my older brothers, and that caused me to act out more. I felt that getting high gave me a voice. I drank so much Colt 45 that I should have stock in the company. I did not care about school anymore, and I got suspended from school twice. By that time my reputation was not good, and I wanted nothing to do with God. Everyone around me got one of two things from me: you would either see my anger or you would get cussed out.

I lost the trust of my mother because of my heavy drinking. She watched me like a hawk as a result of it. I am truly sorry for what I put her through, as well as anybody else that I hurt along the way. I am so sorry, and I pray for forgiveness. When I look back on what I have been through, I can say only that God has been everywhere that I have been. It was not easy for me.

I got out of junior high by the skin of my teeth and thought to myself, "OK, high school, here I come." I had never been around so many beautiful Black women in my life. When the bell rang to change classes, they came from everywhere—all shapes and all sizes. All the guys and some teachers would stand around and just look at all of them. I would say to myself, "My goodness, I just want one." Nothing was changing for me; I was just in a different location, still trying to figure out this thing called life. As time went on, substance abuse increased. It went from drinking to pill popping, and something had to be done. I call it a voice that had to be heard. I felt like I did not matter, so drinking made me have confidence, which was the craziest thing I could imagine at the time.

How many of you know that behind every drug is a spirit? It has one thing in mind, and that is to kill you. The KJLV John 10:10 says, "Lucifer does not care about you at all, he hates God's creation, which includes you and your family. He is angry because he could not dethrone God." Talk about someone with a chip on his shoulder. If you do not have any knowledge of this, you just keep moving, and that is exactly what I did. Time went on, and before I knew it, everybody around me was gone. I asked myself, "What do you do now? You can either get yourself together or keep on destroying yourself." It was time to make a choice, so I decided to try to finish school.

I asked my mother if I could go to a concert after school, and she, surprisingly, said yes. That was my first and my last concert. The bands were called The Softones and First Class. Going to the concert gave me a sense of independence. I watched the show intensely, excited to finally get a chance to see what it was like to sing live. That was short lived—the concert was stopped due to the enormous smell of marijuana. Even if you did not smoke it, you got a contact high from it. The auditorium was filled with so much smoke that you could not even see, but that was OK with me because I got to go .

I left feeling wonderful and rejuvenated, thinking that I could start living without having someone chaperoning me everywhere I went. After all, I was in the tenth grade, and when you are coming of age, you need space to a certain extent. Growing up in the hood, you are exposed to a lot of things. For example, I was seeing people doing drugs, robberies, sex, and fights. That is just a normal day in the hood. I took the dice from my Monopoly game and carved them into the pavement to smooth the edges so that I could make some money shooting craps, and then I realized that I had to put the dice back. I bought another pair to return to the game, but there was a problem: the dice that I took from the game were white and the ones that I put back were red; but the store only had that color, so I took my chances. Nevertheless, that did not work out too well.

I was trying to be one of the boys, trying my hardest to fit in. If you are not accepted, just maybe you are cut out to be a leader at some point in your life. Going into my last two years of high school, I met three ladies who came from Coppin State University. They came to the school to recruit students to join their university. By this time, I had a clear head and a sense of direction regarding what I wanted to do with my life. During my lunch break, I stayed in the room with them and talked about life and what I wanted to do next. They asked me about college, and I said, "Who, me?" and they said, "Yes, you." No one had ever asked me that question before, so I went back to class with a great expectation about my future. However, my reputation was not good among the faculty, so I did not think that I had a chance. I was told, to my face, that I was not going to amount to anything. What a thing to say to an eighteen-year-old kid who was just trying to find his way in this mean world. Who says words do not hurt? Especially when they come from the director of a department of a school that is supposed to help you, not tear you down. A part of this was my fault, but even if you are thinking it, as a professional you should not say it, period. By this time I was used to dealing with being rejected by people. The ladies, however, never gave up on me. They were there for three days, and every chance that I got to say hi, I took it gleefully. They asked me if I could get a copy of my transcript, and I did. They took the time to walk me through the application process, took me out, and bought me a souvenir. What I did not know was that they were students themselves. They asked me if I would like to come to the university and share my experience with their classmates, and I said yes. I thought that was the least that I could do, considering all that they did for me. It went well, and then we said goodbye.

While all this was taking place, I went back to praying and reading again. Every time I come back to the Lord, my life changes for the better. Why does man continuously go back and forth? Two reasons: his flesh is weak (Matt. 26:41), or he is not grounded in the word enough to always remember that we walk away from the Lord, not him from us. Coming back to the Lord gave me a sense of peace and confidence that you can only receive from him.

To my surprise, a month later I received a letter of acceptance from Stillman College in Tuscaloosa, Alabama. When I told my family, I was immediately shut down by my pops. I did not understand it then, but I do now. When your parents are doing everything to protect you from this world, they are doing you a great disservice; still, though, that does not necessarily mean they are bad parents. When you have a child who has the capability of learning and understanding at his or her own pace, there is nothing that you can do about it except to pray and ask God to guide them and protect them. When it is time for them to fly the coop, they are going to do it whether they are ready or not, especially when they see their siblings moving forward without them.

I went back to school the next day, and something else happened. Between classes I was approached by a gentleman in the hallway who said that he was a gym teacher and asked me if I would be interested in wrestling. I said, "Man, that I am not down with. Men sticking their hands in between men's legs."

He said, "It is not what you think. Here me out. I have been watching you, and you remind me of a schoolmate of mine who had no legs. He became a state champion, and I see that in you." I stood there not knowing what to say, and it seemed like time stood still. Eventually, he told me to just come down to the gym after school and he would see what he could do, and that I may be able to get a scholarship.

That is my second regret in life. When the Lord is opening doors, you must walk through them. These opportunities only come around once in a lifetime. I continued to pursue the Lord with everything. In my reading his words, I enjoyed my time with him and enjoyed school as well. I joined the school newspaper club; I had two years left, and I was trying to make the best of the time that I had. By now my family had moved to a better neighborhood, where I knew nobody. I stayed focused because I was in a good place in my life at the time, and I was on fire for the Lord.

I started having dreams again, and this time they did not stop. They were recurring dreams of me being in a stadium as I looked around. The people were coming from everywhere, and I was standing on a platform with the Bible in my hand, telling them to come to Jesus. I told myself it was just a dream and to keep it moving. All that I wanted was more of Jesus.

I met my man David and his family that same year. We clicked instantly; he could sing, and he was the first person that I saw that could handle the rock. He could see the play before it started developing. That is when I said to myself, "That brother got skills." However, our time was short lived. I enjoyed every minute with his family, especially his grandmother. She was the loveliest person one could have ever met. She was always singing or humming to the Lord. She watched me coming home from school every day.

One day she asked me to come in and have a seat with her. She was always sitting by the window. What I did not know was that she could see into the spirit realm, and that was why she was always happy. I came in to have a seat, and she asked me, "What would you do if the Lord healed you?" I said that I did not know. She was the first person that I knew that could see into the spirit realm. She never talked about anything, but Lord, you just knew that something was different about her. How she worshipped, it was like she knew where she was going after her life was over, and she was looking forward to seeing the king of kings. She had two daughters that were on fire as well. Believe me when I tell you we were at every church function—you name it, we were there.

One weekend the members of their family and I went to a lake in Columbia, Maryland, to have some family time. Everybody was having a good time when, suddenly, things changed. I was watching everybody playing in the water, and I decided to take a step forward. The water came to my ankle, so I said to myself, "Cool, I got this." I decided to take one more step, and down I went. I went all the way to the bottom and began to panic. On my way down, I heard this small voice say, "Whatever you do, don't open your mouth." With bulging eyes, I began looking at what was around me. What took a second seemed like a lifetime. The water had a dirty, brownish color to it. A young lady started pushing me toward the top, but I began pulling her down. As we managed to reach the surface, our eyes met. She told me to just hold on and that she was right there.

Down I went again, this time not to the bottom. I was just trying to hold on for dear life—that was all I could think about at the time. My instincts began to kick in, and as I looked in front of me, there she was coming toward me again. This time I grabbed her with everything I had, and she pushed me toward the surface again. She told me to hold on and that she was going to get help. I was going back down again when, out of nowhere, someone scooped me right up out of the water and laid me on the rocks. Three guys were sitting on the edge of the water looking at me. I began thanking the young man who pulled me out. I asked him if there was anything that I could do for him, and he said no. He said, "I had no idea that you were drowning, we were watching you the whole time, and we thought that you were doing the back-stroke." That was my first encounter with death, and it would not be my last.

The ride home was very quiet. I never got a chance to thank her for risking her life just to save mine. I moved on with my daily life like nothing happened. Back to school I went. I started to enjoy my last two years of high school, accompanied by the grace of God. This time I was on fire for the Lord, standing on the corner and passing out tracks while talking to people about God. I would tell them, if they were not going to read the track, to please give it back to me because someone needed it more than they knew. I was very serious about that; I had a burning desire to serve the Lord at any cost. I miss those days. If God turned his back on us as a nation, where would we be?

Moving forward, the one year that I had left was something to remember. The dreams continued, and I was trying to finish strong, not realizing that God was already moving on my behalf, even if I could not see it. Graduation day was approaching, and that day was so unreal to me. I was not supposed to make it at anything because of my disability and lack of education, but God had his hands on me. Trust me, when God has an assignment for you to do, nothing can stop it; there may be some delays, but God is looking for people that he can trust. I was standing in the civic center with four hundred of my classmates, stunned and saying to myself, "Am I dreaming or is this happening?" I did not know the school song, not even to this very day.

Everything was happening so fast. As we continued with the ceremony, rows of students began moving toward the front of the stage to receive their diplomas. That was a sight to see. It took time for the row that I was in to move, so when it was time for us, I said to myself, "Here we go." While we were moving toward the stage, I felt nervous and excited at the same time. They had called my name for the interfaith award when suddenly this loud noise erupted. I asked myself what that was, and the guy behind me told me it was for me and to keep moving. I looked over my right shoulder to see what the noise was, and to my surprise, everybody in the civic center was standing and applauding me as I received my diploma. Who gets a standing ovation at his high school graduation? God, when the Lord is in it, expect the unexpected. That night was surreal. As I was walking off the stage, people began to shake my hand, and all I could say was "God bless you." The night was still young, and as we drove home, nothing was said—not even "Do you want to go anywhere?" and not even a congratulations. I was just dropped off, and Father went on his merry way.

Only a year before this, I watched my sister go to her graduation and to her prom. I watched everything that went into the events for her to have a wonderful evening. I do not mean to slight her in any way. I just think that I should have been given the same consideration. Just because I was different did not mean that I should have been ignored. My overarching point is that people's perception of you can be wrong, even in your own family.

MY VOICE AND MY DREAMS

My high school days were done, and I was wondering where to go from there. With no survival skills or any type of vocational training, what was I to do? I did not have a clue. What I did have, however, was a burning desire to succeed. After watching both of my parents continue to work into their later years, I decided to take some time off. I later regretted that decision, but my parents did not seem to mind. My dreams continued, and again, I did not tell anyone. Who would believe me? I knew that my parents were not going to be here forever, and all that I had was God and my voice.

My days consisted of cleaning, exercising, and praising the Lord. One day I went back to the camp that I had attended as a kid. It was called Camp Green Top. Camp Green Top was a camp for children and adults with disabilities. This time I came back to work as a counselor's aide, and for me, it was nice to see some of the people that I had gone to school with. I was not welcomed back with open arms by some of the guys. I did not know why, but I had a suspicion that it was because I did not stay in touch with anyone. The only thing I wanted to do now was to make some money—that was my mindset.

People with disabilities want the same things in life that normal people want: money, homes, children, ladies, and cars. We talk about the American dream among ourselves, but we are different.

We live in two worlds: one where everybody has a physical or mental disability, and one where nobody does but you. That is what society does not see. What we need is for several organizations to come together to discuss the needs of people with different problems than the ones faced every day—such as one's identity, job, and health care—and to be looked at as people. We know that is not going to happen because of the political bylaws of these organizations. It is all about the money. I have mine to get, and you have yours to get, just to coin a phrase.

What would happen if all these organizations were under one umbrella? A lot more people would get a better chance at life. I experienced chaos with these organizations; for example, people not showing up on time. When they did, they did not want to do any work. Some would also have unprofessional phone etiquette. If you do not have a heart for helping people, please consider a career change because you are affecting someone's life.

I remember when I was assigned to the cutest little curly-haired girl. At the mess hall, when it was time to eat, the first thing that I noticed was that she was blind. Before I met her, I was told that she would not eat for anyone, but they still wanted me to give it a try. The moment that she heard my voice, she began to eat, which made my day because I knew she would eat for me every time she heard my voice. That was all I cared about. Every time that she would hear my voice, she would smile and eat. That was a good time in my life, and that camp is where I met my first girlfriend.

After we did our jobs as aides, the evenings belonged to us. The night was still young, and there were a lot of things happening under the moonlight. Everybody would wake up the next day with smiles on their faces, and every night was a good night. The next day went well; I had a lot of questions for the young lady that I had just met. To my surprise, she lived a block away from members of my family, and I also came to find that she grew up with members of my family. Who would have thought that this was going to happen to me? I had a chance to spend time with my girlfriend and to see my family too. I was nineteen and ready to face the world, or so I thought. Boy was I wrong. The years that I wasted.

Five years not living as a saved individual and back in the world, I was doing nothing but repeating the same thing. This time I was on my own. I had left home looking for what I thought was going to be fun. I was given a key to my aunt's house. I was now a man, staying out all night long doing things that I had no business doing. What I learned was how people in the hood live. Some of the nicest people live in the hood. You grow up fast, and if you are not accepted, they will run you right out of there. Everybody knows the code of the streets—I see nothing, hear nothing, and mind my own business. Things are constantly moving in the hood, inside or out. I called it Little New York, where everybody is trying to get their hustle on. As with everything else in life, every season has its endings (Eccles. 3:17).

A few years later, I had to make a major decision because history was repeating itself. One day I met a guy who became my best friend at the time. This young man was on fire for the Lord. Every time that I think about him now, I say to myself, "Wow, this young man was way before his time." We hit it off right away. We would sit in his room for hours talking about the Lord. He introduced me to Pastor R.W. Schambach, Evangelist A.A. Allen, and Pastor Kenneth E. Hagin.

At that time, I knew nothing about these powerful men of God. He would tell me about the spirit realm and how real it was. When he talked about these things, he had my undivided attention. You could see the love and joy that he had for the Lord in his eyes. At times we would take walks around the neighborhood, and he would say, "The angels are all around us; don't you see them?"

I would say, "No, man, I don't see any angels." We would keep walking. I was in awe of his love for the Lord. After all, we were in our early twenties.

I had one foot in and the other foot out. I was not ready to let go of street life. I thought that I was grown and free. But to be transparent, I was drinking and fornicating my ass off. I would rest up for two weeks at home and exercise like crazy, as if I were in training for an event, just to repeat the cycle over again. Around that time, I realized that everybody around me was in the first-month club, meaning waiting on the first of the month for money from the government rather than working.

One hot summer I was sitting on the steps around 11:00 a.m. when the mailman delivered the mail. Ten minutes later the people started to disappear from both sides of the street. I sat there for a minute, then got up to ask my girlfriend's mother, "Where did everybody go?" She told me it was the first of the month. By that time, my girlfriend had entered the room, and she asked me if I had a check. I told her to give me a minute and that I would be right back. I went to my aunt to ask what was up with this check thing, and she said, "You don't get a check?" I told her I did not. After giving the subject some thought, I also began receiving a check. In my heart, I always wanted more, and I still do, to this day.

After getting tired of doing the same thing repeatedly, I would go home for two weeks at the end of every month to see my mother and reevaluate what I was going to do with the rest of my life. Five years had passed, and I was now twenty-three. I would go home and create real-life people in my head, like basketball legend Dominique Wilkins and boxer Marvelous Marvin Hagler. I would watch them constantly—news clippings and anything I could find. To me, a man can only have hope if he sees something greater than himself, so these men became my heroes. I knew that I would never meet these men, so after asking the Lord for direction, I decided to go to school. This is why I always say to never give up and to just keep fighting, no matter what you are faced with. Trust me when I say I am living proof that a door is going to open when you least expect it to (Matt. 7:7).

I began to make a change after crying out to the Lord for help. He tasted alcohol from me, and there I was going back to church. I knew well enough that the Lord will never leave you; we leave him (Deut. 31:6–8). I was back where I belonged, or so I thought. One day in church, I went up for prayer, and the pastor said, "How can I help you?" So I said, "I think I am called to preach." What happened next broke me into pieces. He said, "Good, son," and pushed me on. I was devastated. After all, I was a member of the church. This man baptized me in the basement of the church on a Sunday night in March of 1979. Before he dipped me into the water, he said, "If this young man comes back up out this water healed, don't you all run out of this church." Of course, though, that did not happen.

I found myself wondering what to do from there. I just did not know anymore. After much continuous prayer, I decided to enroll in Washington Bible College in 1983 and was accepted. After all that I was going through up to this point in my life, all that I had to go on was my faith. Once I received my letter of acceptance, I told my girlfriend and some members of her family. Their response was disbelief, because I was not living the life of a Christian in front of them but, rather, one of a hypocrite.

I remember going home and telling my parents the good news. My mother did not say anything. But my father had a lot to say. He said he had never heard of the school or its location. I thought to myself, "Here we go again." I also asked myself why I always received so much opposition from him at every turn. What he said was law—nobody ever challenged his authority. I did not have a say, and I just could not understand why I was not allowed to have an opinion in his eyes. After all, it was my life that we were talking about. I did not find out until decades later, when my oldest brother was talking in retrospect about our lives with our father, that our father did not want me to work. This had led my brother to contact our father to discuss my situation. I asked my brother what he had said to him, and he said, "Old man, let him go. He will never experience life or learn anything if you keep sheltering him."

From that day forth, my father let me make my own decisions. He also famously said, "If my son comes to you about a major decision, he is just asking for your opinion."

Weeks were still ahead of me before it was time for me to attend college, so I tried to spend as much time with my girlfriend as I could. One night I was standing on the corner talking, and my pastor pulled up at the red light. He waved to me, and I waved back. The church was around the corner from where I was standing.

The weeks flew by, and before I knew it, the morning came for me to leave. I had already been to the school for orientation and a campus visit. Everything went well, but one thing that came to my mind was the look on my mom's face when it was time for me to leave. She experienced an array of emotions. We got there, and I went up to the dorm. I looked around, and my father put down my suitcase. We said our goodbyes, and I looked around some more, then sat at my desk, showing no emotion whatsoever.

An hour later, my pastor and his son walked into my room. We looked at each other, and the pastor asked if I was who he'd seen some months ago standing on the corner. I confirmed that I was, and then he asked me what I was doing there. He had come to drop off his son, whom I had seen a few times in church but did not know personally. After we both settled in, we exchanged a few words and went to dinner.

Once dinner was over, I was asked if I would like to keep score at the basketball game that night. Of course, I said yes. We lost that night, but I enjoyed the experience of being that close while watching a real live college game from the floor. After the game, we all went back to the dorm to get ready for the next day. On my first day of classes, two college professors left a lasting impression on me that stands to this day: Dr. Kim, who was all business and wanted you to know all the books of the Bible in chronological order by the next day, and Dr. Fowler. When Dr. Fowler talked about the glory of God, he left you in amazement.

Everything was going well that first week. Before long, however, I could not sleep at night. I wondered what was going on, because I had never had this problem before. I was falling asleep at five in the morning and had to be in the classroom at eight, so I pushed through it as much as I could. There were days when I was just trying to adjust, which became extremely difficult at that time. I was not prepared for what was ahead, like not having enough food to eat on the weekends or money to get by. Things started to break me down. I was falling behind in my studies and got into a physical altercation with one of my classmates. For the latter, I was called into the office and asked how I was going to pay for my tuition for the year. So I asked for work-study jobs on campus and was told that there was not anything available. They did tell me that I could go out into the community and find a job. Before leaving, I asked how much I owed. I was told my tuition was four thousand a year. I had not told anyone that I did not come from money, so I had to decide what my next move would be quickly.

In the coming weeks, something happened that broke my spirit. I was walking out of a classroom to go to another classroom. As I walked toward the door, I noticed that there was no handrailing for me to get up the steps to the door to the next hall. I had to take my book bag and put it around my neck, then bend over to put my right hand on one step and push my body forward until I reached the top of the stairs to open the door myself. That part did not bother me—I did what I had to do at that time—but there was something that did bother me. The students were walking on both sides of me going into the same building, and not one of them offered to help me. Some of them decided to make things worse. Some of those students lived in the same dorm as me. That was when I said that I was done. I felt so humiliated.

The next day I went to administration and told them that I wanted out. They told me to have a seat. I was in front of a committee that was trying to convince me to stay. They asked me what the problem was, so I said that I was falling behind in my studies. They began to tell me what they could do for me, which was to assign a person to help with my studies. I immediately said no thanks, and they began to tell me the story of a former student that I reminded them of. His grades never went beyond a D, so they suggested that he audit his classes, to which he complied. They also told me that he now had a congregation of three thousand people. I was not moved by their attempt to make me stay, so they pulled one more last-ditch effort to try to convince me to change my mind.

They asked me to call my mother, which surprised me at the time, but I did. The conversation with her was very brief. I told them that I was a grown man and that the decision was mine to make. What should I have told them? There was a lot more going on with me than just my grades. At that time, all that I was thinking about was that I wanted out.

With the weekend quickly approaching, I decided it was my time to leave. I did not even say goodbye to any of the guys. My father and I had started walking toward the car, not saying a word to each other, when suddenly I heard someone calling my name. I turned around and saw that it was the same guy that I'd had the altercation with. He asked me if there was anything that he could say or do to convince me to stay. I politely told him no. He asked me if I was sure, to which I told him yes and left.

After driving a few miles on the road, my father asked me who that was and what that was all about. I began to tell him some of the things that had happened to me, but then no more was said. I found out years later that my mother and grandmother had been so very proud of me for attending school. The person who told me was a client of my mothers who became like a second mother to me. To my mom, I am so sorry that I let her and the other members of the family down, for I truly did not know.

DEALING WITH DISAPPOINTMENT BUT MOVING ON

I was back home again but refused to give up. Nobody asked me any questions about my experiences, and everybody was still doing the same old thing, what seemed to be the same things on repeat. I then began to realize my frustration with wanting to be successful. It was not going to be easy. I heard of a school called Baltimore School of the Bible. I enrolled, thinking once more, here we go again. The requirements were to pick the courses that you gravitated toward, and upon finishing the semester, you would receive a certificate of completion. I started well, but my heart was not in it. The truth of the matter was that I wanted a job. I was tired of the college thing. I'd had enough. But I would not trade any of my experiences for the world, even though some of my memories were not always good. My bad memories drove me to succeed even more.

One day I held my girlfriend in my arms and told her to just hold on. I told her that I was going to get us out of the toxic environment we were in, and I kept my promise to her. Out of nowhere, something wonderful happened that would change our lives forever. We were watching the local news when the reporter began talking about a groundbreaking story. The story was about a brand-new senior citizen building in a wonderful area of the city.

I took the information down, and off I went to see if I met the criteria to have my first apartment. I did the interview, which went well, and the process was fairly easy. I did not say anything because I wanted to see if it would go through. What took months seemed like years. One day a letter came in the mail saying that I was approved for an apartment. I accepted. Then the time came to tell my parents. With a look of disbelief on his face again, my father, oddly, became very supportive. He already knew that I was very determined to succeed in everything I put my mind to.

When people with disabilities accomplish something, no matter how great or small, it is a major accomplishment for us. For example, when we obtain a job or drive a car. Things do not always come as easy for us as they would for the average person. I would love to know how it feels to walk down a flight of stairs without holding on to a rail or to be able to stand up and put on my pants one leg at a time. Please do not take things for granted.

The time came for me to move into my first apartment, and off we went. We had nothing but our clothes and blankets. We slept on the floor until we were able to buy furniture. Eventually, we got a sofa bed and a chair. There we were, starting a new chapter in our lives. We kept a low profile because my girlfriend was not on the lease. The rules stated that you could have a guest for two weeks upon notifying the office. When we moved in and out, some people began to complain about her staying there, but they would never confront me about it.

One night during our monthly meeting, I approached the district manager and asked to meet with her to discuss my circumstances. She took me into the manager's office. During the conversation, I told her that I knew what the rules about guests were, and then I told her that we were young and asked her if she remembered what that was like. After listening to a few more things that I had to say, she decided to let me have an extra key.

You see, living with senior citizens is not always easy. For one thing, there is a huge generational gap. I was raised to respect my elders, but what I had come to find was that some of them were not as nice and sweet as you would think. I will give some examples. Some of them thought that we were not a good fit. I was told to my face by one man that he did not want us there. Some of them sold drugs, and there was a loan shark in the same building. Some of them were creeping in the night from apartment to apartment. When you saw them the next day, they acted like nothing ever happened and had nothing but nice things to say, which made me look at them sideways.

The truth of the matter was that, when it came to screening, management needed to do a better job by ruling with an iron fist. You cannot be timid when dealing with people and their families. I was not always a saint, but for the most part, I just wanted to be left alone. I do have great memories of some nice people. After all, I lived in that building for seventeen years, so I am not trying to paint a bad picture. People are just people. With that being said, I would have changed some of my experiences there, but for what it is worth, it was not all bad.

Years later I was informed by my longtime girlfriend that she was pregnant. What we felt at that time was indescribable. After a decade of being together, when we found out, I remember nothing was said because both of us were in shock. That wore off fairly quickly; we were about to be parents, and she was so happy. A lot of our friends who were disabled already had children, so she thought she would fit right in.

We had never talked about having children. Then one day, she came home from her routine doctor visit, and I asked her how it had gone. She proceeded to say that she'd had a thorough examination and that she wanted me to get checked out as well. She would like to start a family. After listening to her, I told her that I would.

I made an appointment to see a urologist, and when that day came, the visit was quick and straight to the point. After filling out standard paperwork, I was taken into a waiting room. Two minutes later the doctor came into the room and introduced himself to me. To this day I cannot remember his name. I told him why I was there, but what happened next, I was not ready for. I told the doctor that my girlfriend had received a clean bill of health and that I was not circumcised. He then told me he was going to look to see what the problem was. He reached for the small stool, put on plastic gloves, and told me to pull my pants down.

He then proceeded to pull back on my penis, to which I said, "Wait a minute, doc, this isn't a toy." To that, he said, "I barely touched you. The problem is that you have too much foreskin around the head of your penis, which causes a blockage of the semen when you ejaculate. You need to be circumcised."

I asked when we could have it done, and to my surprise, he said next week. I asked him who would be doing the surgery, to which he said that he would, and he would have his receptionist schedule me an appointment for next week. In addition to this, he told me to take a plastic container for a semen count as well as to check for bacteria. He said it was standard procedure—for me to put the container into a brown bag with no exposure to light—and that he would see me next week.

I went home and called my father to ask him if he could take me next week. He said that he could and that he would be there at five before ten, which meant, in his mind, that I needed to be ready before nine fifty. He was a stickler for time, and if you were not ready, you were going to hear about it from him.

Can you imagine what was going through my mind on the day of the surgery? I was trying to masturbate with my father downstairs waiting for me. As expected, that took some time. It takes some time in a man's head. You have to take yourself there even though there is no woman in front of you physically. You can, however, bring her there mentally. You remember the old saying—a mind is a terrible thing to waste.

I was going out my front door late, knowing full well I would have to explain why I was so late. As I began to open the car door, I said hi to my dad and began to put one leg in. Before I could do or say anything else, he asked what took me so long. I told my dad I had to jerk off as per the doctor's orders, and that was what the brown bag had in it. He then said, "You had to do what you had to do." I repeated everything over so that he would understand, then he said, "Don't no son of mine have to jerk off, and why didn't your mother have this done for you early?" He was not happy. He told me he would have to talk to my mother about this. What he did not realize was the whole picture—when the doctors told her that her son was not breathing, she was not thinking about a procedure at the time.

He dropped me off, and I was taken into a waiting room where the doctor and his staff were waiting. We said good morning to each other, then the doctor began to explain what was about to take place. He asked me to please get up on the table. I noticed two guys at the end of the table, which I thought was strange. They were just standing there. What the doctor said next, I was not ready for. He told me they were going to tie my legs and arms apart, and before I could say anything, it was done, and I was tied like an X.

I thought that I was going to be put to sleep, but then he said what he was about to do next. "I am going to give you six injections in your scrotum for pain. When the pain starts to come on, put up your finger, and I'll administer another shot." What I heard next was a sound that I was too familiar with—the sound of that dreaded drill took me back to my surgery days. I hated those days, and to this very day, I still do.

As the pain started coming on, I raised my finger. To my surprise, I heard the doctor say, "I can't give you any more injections."

What seemed like an eternity only took a few more minutes, and then it was over. They helped me off the table and into the doctor's office for more instructions and to make a follow-up appointment. He told me that he was going to prescribe me Tylenol and codeine for pain, just enough for a week, and that I would experience some pain when I was trying to pass urine. He also said that I would want to take warm baths, which would cause my stitches to fall off, and that he would see me in a week.

Life was back to normal, and everything the doctor said was going to happen did, but one thing he did not mention was the incredible erections that I would receive from this. For a whole week I experienced pain trying to pass my urine or from erections.

Before I knew it, it was time to go back to see the doctor. I was sitting in the waiting room when he walked in and said, "Good morning, sir. I have the results of your test. We found a little bit of bacteria, but that is normal. I have another question for you.

Are you an addict?"

"Nah, man, why?"

"Because the prescription that I prescribed for you should have lasted you more than a week."

I said that I was not counting, and I was just trying to stop the pain. That seemed to appease him because from there we continued as normal. He told me everything looked fine and to go home and use it. That is exactly what I did, and within two or three months, my girlfriend was pregnant.

WHAT IN HELL AM I GOING TO DO?

When I found out that she was pregnant, my body and mind went numb. We were about to be parents. The first thing that came to my mind was that I must get a job. I also wondered where we were going to live. We could not stay in a senior citizens' building because children were not allowed into that type of setting. There was only one other building that we knew of, less than a mile away from where we were. We knew of couples that I went to school with that lived in that building and had children. The parents were disabled, but their children were born healthy and were very successful. To get in there was a never-ending waiting list, so in my mind, time was of the essence, and we had to do something immediately. It turned out that it was not as simple as I thought.

My second priority was to make sure that the baby and my girlfriend were fine. All seemed well, and we were happy. She never missed a prenatal appointment. I was in disbelief and excited toward the future. Of course, the gossiping seniors were saying they could not believe she was pregnant and were complaining about me not having a job. They had some nerve. I am sure they said a lot of other things, but they never said anything to me or my girlfriend when they saw us. It is funny how people think that they have all the answers for your life but do not have control of their own lives whatsoever.

As we continued to process that we were about to have a baby, out of nowhere, my oldest brother showed up. You see, my father had sons by different women, which meant that my brothers and I did not see each other very often. When my brother would show up, he always made sure that I had everything I needed, because there was a high probability that I would not see him for months, or even years, afterward. Regardless, there he was looking dapper, as always, with a beautiful woman by his side. They seemed to be happy. Even though he came to see the whole family, I always felt he came just for me—that is how much love he had, and still has, for me. I always looked up to him, and he became my hero.

Standing in front of us was a wonderful person, who came into our lives. Words cannot express what she meant to us, and still does to this very day. To Nora, let me first say thank you so much for the joy that you brought into our lives. You are exactly what we needed at that time. Being in your presence was like a breath of fresh air, and I hope that wherever you are, this book finds you and finds you well.

My son's name was Terrell. He was born prematurely; he was only three pounds and two ounces. When I saw him, it seemed like time stood still. The nurse saw that I looked like I was in shock, so she began to tell me it was going to be all right. We just wanted him to get healthy enough that we could take him home. My girlfriend went to the hospital to see him every day, and then I started going too. I remember one time we were in the room when the nurses station announced a code blue over the PA system, which meant that everyone needed to stay put. After everything calmed down, I asked a passing nurse what a code blue meant. She told me that when you hear that, it means a baby is dying. In the time that we spent coming and going, when we would hear code blue, it made me sick to my stomach.

We went to see him midweek one time, and we found out that he had been moved to another room. When we got to the new room, we met a young lady who left a lasting impression on us. As we walked into the room, her baby was crying and shaking profusely. I introduced myself but could not keep my eyes off her son. He looked like he was in so much pain that I felt compelled to ask why he was crying nonstop. To this, I was told he was going through withdrawal, as if it were nothing. What she said next, I was not ready for. She asked me if she could have my candy bar. I was done.

After that encounter we were ready to leave, but we kept our focus on our son, whom we could not wait to see. The next day we went right back to see him again. This time the ICU nurse came to tell me that he could hear me, so I began to talk to him. I told him to hold on and that I was right there. What I did next I still talk about to this very day. As I continued to talk to him, I stuck my finger in through the side of the incubator, into his little hand. To my surprise, he began to squeeze my finger. That was his way of letting me know he knew I was there, and that moment was when my heart broke into little pieces. I still get emotional when I think about it.

The next day my mother came. I remember the nurse saying, "So you're the grandmother!" and my mother replying, "Yes, I am." The nurse asked if she would like to hold him, and to that, my mother said, "Oh no, I'll wait until he gets some size to him." I often wonder if this was déjà vu for her. First her son, and now her grandson. We didn't talk about it.

One thing was for sure, though. When the hospital told my girlfriend that she could spend the night with him, she was so happy. Like any other mother, she did not want to leave him. I wish they had told her that earlier.

We got the call one evening. The phone rang, and when I answered, the nurse said no greeting. She only asked for the parents of Terrell to come to the hospital right away. Before I could put the phone down, my girlfriend was completely out the door. I called my boy down the hall from me and asked his girlfriend if she could take me to the hospital (she was a nurse). She told me that she would meet me in the lobby of our building, and off we went. We had to go completely across town, so we hit the expressway doing eighty and with nothing being said. Halfway down the expressway, I told my friend to slow down, and she asked me why.

I told her I could tell he was gone, and she told me not to say that. This exchange made her drive faster.

When we got there, she dropped me off, and I went straight to the nurses' station. They were waiting for me, and we began to walk down a hall that I was not familiar with. There were no other nurses, and the atmosphere felt like it was as quiet as the vacuum of space. By this time, I knew something had changed because it felt so different.

I was taken into this sitting room, where the first thing I noticed was a priest standing to my right. He looked at me, and I looked to my left, and then I heard a nurse saying, "We have to take him now." My girlfriend walked in holding onto him for dear life and with tears running down her face. My eyes went directly toward him. There he was, paper white, with no life in him at all. He was gone, and at that moment, all I could do was scream in anguish. That was one of the worst days of my life.

The hospital said that it was his heart. It is amazing how things can suddenly change overnight. After that type of heartbreak, what do you do? All I wanted to do was stop the pain that I was feeling. That night a part of me died, and I was just going through the motions. I began to drink even heavier than before in a vain attempt to numb the pain. To this very day, nobody from either of our families ever talks about what we went through. No. "I am sorry for your loss" or "If you need to talk, I am here." When I talk about the children within the family and I mention his name, I always get the response of "Who?" as if he never existed. I can tell you one thing for certain, as long as I am alive, he will never be forgotten.

We went home to make funeral arrangements for the following week. When we got to the funeral home, my mother, my girlfriend, and I were waiting to say our goodbyes. Suddenly, someone in the funeral home approached me just to say, "He's not here yet." I said, "What in the hell do you mean he's not here yet?" To this, he said, "Sir, we sent someone to pick up his body, but they forgot him, so we had to send them back to pick him up." By this time, I was livid. Who forgets to put a baby in their casket at a funeral?

My mother told me to calm down, that it was going to be all right, and that she was sorry she could not stay because she was already late for work.

There we were, waiting for them to return with his body. It was not too long after that when I saw them coming in with him. Before they let us see him, we were told that in the back of the building, there was a little cemetery for children. They allowed us to say our last goodbyes. I could not muster the strength to speak, but my girlfriend did. We went home and tried to move forward with our lives. My heart hurts when I think about what my girlfriend went through.

Just a few weeks later, on a Monday morning, we got up to start our day. I was in the kitchen, and my girlfriend was in the bedroom getting dressed for church. I asked her what she was doing and told her that it was Monday and there was no church on Monday. She adamantly said once more that she had to go to church. By this time, I knew something was wrong, so I picked up the telephone and called my friend down the hall from me. I told her what was going on with my girlfriend, and she said that she would be right there. I walked around my girlfriend to open the front door. My friend came in, took a single look at my girlfriend, and my girlfriend fainted. My friend picked up the phone and called 911. After this, my friend took my girlfriend's vital signs until EMS arrived.

Off we went to the hospital. I was right by her side. When we got there, they took her and began to run all kinds of tests. This process took all morning and half of the afternoon. Around two, the doctors let us see her. The nursing staff kept constantly approaching my friend, asking if she would like to come and work for them. Of course, she declined every time. The doctor asked us to step out of the room with him, and he told us that they had run a series of tests but could not find anything wrong with my girlfriend. He asked if she'd had any trauma in her life lately, and I told him that we just lost a son. He determined from there that she was suffering from postpartum depression.

They released her to us, and we took her home. We tried to get back to a somewhat normal life, but we both knew things would never be the same. We both needed healing. For a while, things started going back to normal. We both got part-time jobs, and it worked out well for her but not for me. My mindset was two things: getting a job and driving. I was not going to let anything stand in the way of me achieving those goals.

V.S.P. Industries sponsored a job fair in all the hotels in the surrounding area, so me and my man went to one of the events. What we did not know was that the television stations were there as well. The rules were we were only allowed to go to two tables, but I had my mind made up—I was going to every table in the place, regardless. I went to my first table, and the sign said Cross Keys Inn. I put in my application, specifically stating that I wanted to work at the front desk. After formally introducing myself, I was asked if I had any front desk experience. I told them the truth, which was that I did not, but I was willing to learn. She said that they needed help in the kitchen and that they could offer me three dollars and thirty-five cents an hour. I excused myself and told her to have a nice day. She told me to wait a minute and upped her offer to four dollars. I made a counteroffer of four-fifty, and she told me I was hired.

As we were leaving, a reporter put a mic into my face and began to ask me to talk about my experience at the job fair. I declined the offer due to fear, but my boy grasped the mic and spoke very well. I was quite surprised by this. After we left, we rushed home to see him on the local six o'clock news.

Before you know it, it was time for me to start my new job. I was introduced to the kitchen staff. We all got along well, and our jobs went smoothly. After three weeks of working there, I was approached by the director of human resources with a gentleman from the local paper saying that they wanted to do a follow-up article on the people who were hired from the job fair. They took some pictures, and as he was writing the article, I leaned forward to tell him to make sure I was quoted correctly. He assured me not to worry; that I could not understand what he was writing because he was writing in shorthand.

I went back to work. A lot of my coworkers were proud, but I was not, because the article mentioned another organization that received credit for helping me. They did not help me find a job or even tell me about the job fair for that matter. I found out about the job fair from watching the local news, so my question for them was: Why are they receiving credit for something that they did not deserve? Especially when I got the job on my own. It is all about funding, and I needed to keep moving, so that is exactly what I did.

My next big goal was to purchase a vehicle, and so I did that as well. I went to vocational rehabilitation to pitch my idea for receiving hand controls for my vehicle, and they said that I would need to prove to them that I needed hand controls when I could use another form of transportation. I also needed to have the car in my name. I told them that I had the car in my name and also that I had full coverage on the vehicle. All that I would need from them was driving lessons to learn to use the hand controls. I obtained my temporary driving license. I began driving lessons shortly after that, which started for me as very exciting until I had to master the turnabout. This step took some time. Months went by before I would get a handle on the turnabout.

The day finally came for me to take the driver's test, and the instructors sent their best. The man who executed my test introduced himself to me as Mr. Cunningham. He told me that he had been looking through my paperwork and noticed that I had several driving instructors with no successful results. He also said that he had thirty years of experience, and that I was going to be driving. I asked where we were going to take the test, and he said Westminster, Maryland. I was confused by this because Westminster was in another county that was at least thirty minutes away. Regardless, there we went, with nothing being said.

As soon as we pulled up to the Bureau of Motor Vehicles building, Mr. Cunningham said that there was a McDonald's across the street and he was going to get some breakfast. He told me, when he came back, that I had better have my license and asked me if I would like some breakfast. I politely declined his offer. Two seconds later, a female state trooper got into the car and said that she would be administering my test. She told me to pull up to the two cones and stop, which I did, and then she told me to do the turnabout. I was doing well until I got to the halfway point and my mind went blank. I forgot everything that I was taught and was panicking in the middle of the driving test.

Feeling an immense amount of anger with myself, I lost all hope. I put the car in park, banged my fist against the steering wheel, and yelled that I quit. The trooper asked me what I'd just said, and I said once more that I quit. To this, she asked if I wanted my license or not. I replied quickly that yes, I did. It was what she said then that changed my life. She said, with a stern look on her face, that this was not about me. I questioned the statement with a strange look on my face.

She said, "This is not just about you. I have a daughter who is fourteen years old, and she has cerebral palsy. One day she is going to want to drive, just like you. So, get it done. Turn the car back on and finish the job. I will see you inside when you are done." I put the car back into reverse, and before I knew it, I was done. It was finally over.

I got out of the car and went into the building to stand in a very short line. I looked toward the counter, and there she was, standing behind the clerks, talking to the next customer, and smiling from ear to ear. Without making a sound, I mouthed the words, thank you. With a thumbs up, she replied a cheery, "You're welcome!"

The clerk called my number next. As I approached the counter, my mind was a thousand times lighter. I was very proud of myself for accomplishing everything I had set out to do. I would like to take the time to thank the Holy Spirit for being there when I needed someone to talk to when nobody else was around, even though it took years to cultivate a relationship between us. I would also like to thank the Holy Spirit for being there when I was doing stupid things, as he never left me (Deut. 31:6). I would also like to thank the state trooper for her help, and Mr. Cunningham as well. They changed my life in so many ways.

I walked out of the building and got back into the car. Mr. Cunningham approached and got back into the car with me. He asked me if I got it. I said yes, and then he took me home. I was waiting for the approval for the hand controls, and before I knew it, everything was finalized and set in stone. I was excited to know what it felt like to be independent instead of relying on other forms of transportation or other people. By this time, I could confidently say that life was good.

One day I could not get a ride to work. I decided that I was going to drive myself but did not have enough road experience. I had to get to work, so I left early. A few weeks later I was coming from the market and making a left turn when I looked up at the sun and lost control of the vehicle. Instead of trying to regain my composure, I pressed down on the hand controls. This made the car accelerate, and before I knew it, I was headed for the median strip. Onto the strip, I went. I said aloud, "Lord, if you don't help me, I'm going to die." I turned the car completely around on the median strip and proceeded to go back into oncoming traffic. While their light was turning green, I jumped the curb and went through a fence before the car came to a complete stop. All of this happened during rush hour traffic.

I was sitting there looking straight ahead when an irate driver walked up to my car, opened the door, and told me that, when I made that turn, I clipped his car. I said that I was sorry and I would make sure he was taken care of. He said he ought to punch me in my face. At that point I reached under my seat like I was reaching for a weapon because I did not know what he was going to do next. He closed the door and backed off.

By this time the police had arrived on the scene and asked me for my license and registration. An officer asked if I had been drinking. I confidently told the officer I had not and that I was very much against drinking and driving. He told me he was going to run my tags and that if I had any outstanding warrants, he was going to throw the book at me. I said, "Officer, do you see that young man right there ranting and raving up and down the sidewalk?" He confirmed that he did, and I told him about the man threatening me. He asked me how the man was threatening me, and I let him know everything. The officer then approached the man and asked him if he was aware that I was disabled, to which he stated, "I don't give a fuck. Look at him; he's sitting straight up. You can't tell." The officer told him with an authoritative tone that if he did not calm down, he was going to arrest him. He then looked over to me and said he would be right back. I kept apologizing profusely to both of them. Out of nowhere I heard a lady screaming, "Oh my goodness! What am I going to tell my husband?"

I was simply sitting there, listening and watching all of this unfold, because I could not get out of the vehicle. I was pinned in the front seat, and the car was up on the curb. Eventually I realized that when I'd made that sharp left turn, I must have clipped two vehicles. I saw my supervisor drive by, and I shouted to him out that I would not be going in to work tomorrow.

The officer returned my information, and I asked him for the young man's phone number. I wanted to make sure that he was all right because he was still visibly angry. By this time the paramedics had arrived, and I said once more that I was so sorry. They quickly told the officer that they were going to get me out of there before I went into shock. They began to pull me out by the passenger side, and the lady who was screaming was sitting and watching the paramedics pull me out of the car.

She said, "Oh my God, he is disabled! I am a nurse; let me help you." To that, I replied, "Ma'am, do not touch me. Your professionalism was not showing a few minutes ago. Do not put your hands on me." They rushed me to the hospital.

As the paramedics were taking me out of the ambulance, standing at the front entrance of the hospital were four nurses waiting to see if I was all right. My girlfriend was there too. I gave them a thumbs up. When the nurses took my vital signs, they said that they were going to get me a tetanus shot and send me on my way. I was relieved, as I was expecting the worst.

I went home. I took a moment to catch my breath, and then I decided to call and see if the young man was feeling any better. What happened next surprised even me. I introduced myself over the phone, attempted once again to apologize for the accident that I'd caused and asked if he was all right. The woman on the phone told me that he was fine and I had just scratched the side of his car. She also said that he had just come in and told her everything. I asked her if he also told her that I had a disability and that he'd threatened me. She did not even tell me to hold on; I could hear her immediately telling him that he should have come to my aid instead of what he had done. Then I heard the clear sound of her hitting him before he could respond. When she stopped, she asked if I was all right. I confirmed that I was, and then we hung up. It was a long time before I drove again.

After several years, my relationship was on its last legs, so we decided to call it quits but continued to respect and help each other as needed. How many curveballs can one take before they shatter? I had concluded that when one is destined for greatness, he or she gets no breaks. I was all alone, telling myself this could not be it. I kept trying until I found what I was looking for. With that being said, years went by, and nothing was happening until I made a call to a friend of mine.

She asked me what I was up to, and I told her that I was bored out of my mind. She asked me why I had not decided to volunteer. I asked her what she meant, and she explained that I could volunteer where I work. I asked her to tell me more. She said the hours were from 8:00 a.m. to 3:00 p.m. Monday through Friday.

I put in for a ride for Monday morning, and off I went. After going through the orientation process, I started the following week. I met some wonderful people whom I miss to this very day. A few of them were Ms. Elaine Mitchell, who I know loved me like I was her son; Ms. Dolores Robinson, who once said to me that I could do anything I put my mind to; Ms. Adrienne Jackson, who always told me that I was something else every time that we talked; Ms. Tia Scott, who nicknamed me "big money grip," and Ms. Patrice Dunaway, who encouraged me to make that call to begin volunteering. I thank them all from the bottom of my heart. Words genuinely cannot express how those ladies and the Department of Social Services changed my life. I also thank all of the men and women of that agency who brought so much joy into my life.

After my fourth year of working at the Department of Social Services, I felt that it was time for me to leave the state of Maryland altogether. I used to stand in the middle of my living room floor periodically and say, "Lord, I have to get out of this city, because if I do not, I am going to be hurt by someone or vice versa." I also stated, "Lord, I do not know how you are going to do it, but I do know that you are going to do it." I never stopped believing those words. Everybody around me had no aspirations to succeed. They seemed to trap themselves right where they were, with no hope or insight to move forward in life. If you are not careful, you too can fall into the same trappings. In a situation such as this, you better learn how to pray. If you do not, you will lose the battle.

A LIFE-CHANGING EVENT

So there I was, contemplating if I should leave or stay. After all, I had finally found a job that I could retire from; all I had to do was put the time in. But I still was not happy with myself. One evening I received a call from my oldest brother out of nowhere, with him telling me that he had somebody that I would want to meet. They had been sitting around discussing the Bible, and my name had come up.

A woman was on the other end of the phone; she introduced herself, and I said hello. Then she immediately began to prophesize. I insulted her gift by asking her if she was a psychic, and to add insult to injury, I said, "All right, Ms. Dionne Warwick, can you find your way to San Jose?" Her reply was, "First of all, I'm not a psychic. I don't like to be called that. And second of all, you got jokes?" She then began to tell me things that were going on inside my apartment that only I could see, as though she were right there with me, even though she was in another state. For example, she said, "Did you just get out of the shower?" and I said, "Yes, I did." I asked myself how she knew that, and then she asked me if a woman was lying across my bed. Once again, I said yes, and then she said that is not the woman for you.

That was my first time dealing with someone with this gift in the body of Christ. Nobody ever told me about the gifts. That happened over forty years ago, and to this very day, we have remained friends. One would think that experience would draw me closer to God, but not me. Man can find pleasure in his sin, but there will come a day when he will be held accountable for his actions.

In the meantime I was still working while waiting for a decision to be made on my one year of personal leave of absence. I felt that my life needed a change. After consulting with a number of my coworkers, some said they would not do it and others said to go for it, saying that you do not get this chance every day. After all, if things did not work out, I would have a year in which I could return to my job.

By this time I was in a relationship with a woman that was out of my league. Let me say this—when you are looking for something you do not need, it will find you. With that being said, I gave up everything I had in hopes that things would change. Why is it that when you meet someone, it always starts well and then spirals out of control? I felt as though I was putting everything into this relationship, and she was doing the minimum. Just because a man has limitations does not mean that he is not a man first.

I was becoming burned out at my job and was not happy in my relationship at the time. The truth of the matter is that I was making too many bad decisions. There were times when I was alone for a very long time. Now I realize that you have to set goals for yourself or history will repeat itself. I was sitting on the steps of the home I was living in, trying to clear my head because I knew that my life was about to change. I received a phone call at the time that I needed it. It was my brother telling me, "Hold on; do not make any decisions that you are going to regret. In a couple of days, you are going to receive a phone call from a young lady." I did not give it too much thought because I had to continue to go to work.

I had too much on my mind at that time, and I was still waiting for the approval of my leave. You see, I had to wait for a few months before human resources would sign off on the approval. I was asked by my supervisor if everything was all right with me because my attendance had improved. She did not realize that the reason it had improved was because that was the only way I could receive the phone call from a young lady I was talking to from Ohio. Because the lady that I was living with would not put up with my taking calls at home. But the woman I was living with was playing me like a fiddle. For example, I would come home from work, and there would be another guy sitting at the dining room table. She was also always in the nightclub, so I became a babysitter.

All that I ever wanted in life was my own family, so what I did was flip the script. I began to do what she was doing to me. I was sleeping with one woman, but my mind was on another. I felt that was my only way out without drawing attention to myself. So I began to play the game too. I did receive that phone call an hour before closing at my job. I said who I was, and she stated who she was and that she had been trying to reach me all day. What my brother did not tell her was that we did not have the same last name, which made it hard for her to find me every time she called. She was told that nobody was here by that name, so she said that she was going to try one more time, and when she did, I received the phone call.

This time the conversation went something like this: "Good afternoon, Social Service West Wood, Mr. Mills speaking. How can I help you?"

"Is there a Darrell Johnson there?"

"No, but my name is Darrell."

"Oh, hi! I have been trying to call you all day. I said that this was going to be my last try for the day."

I then apologized for the miscommunication between us, and she told me that it was OK. I said that I only had thirty minutes before leaving, so my skills were put to the test by trying to answer a ten-line switchboard and talk to her at the same time.

You see, I loved being on the switchboard. What I did was memorize every worker's extension and name by heart. This woman from Ohio already knew a little bit of what I was dealing with in my present relationship, so I just wanted to reiterate my side of the situation to make her feel comfortable. With that being said, we started talking every day, which is why my attendance improved. Talking with her was like a breath of fresh air. I was looking forward to going to work because I gave everything that I had into my relationships, thinking that we could work together when that has not always been the case for me. Knowing that it was time to move on to something new, we continued talking while, strategically, I was about to make a move that would change my future overnight. I became a player. I was so tired of being used.

This is how it went down. She asked, "Would you like to see me?" and I said, "Yes, I would love to see you." So she made the arrangements to make it happen.

There I was, about to take my first vacation in my adult life without my family. I put in for a vacation day for that Friday, and the woman that I was living with said, "You have never taken a vacation in all the years that I have known you, and where did you say you are going?" Then I said, "Florida to see my brother." This was a lie. Why could I not be discreet when playing someone and just be blunt about it? I felt so disrespected, and by this time, I had something to prove. So off I went on my first airplane ride.

I arrived at the airport. They checked my luggage and took me over to the counter to check me in. They treated me like I was royalty. What I did not know was that when you are disabled, they put you on and off the plane first. That must be company policy. So there I was, waiting for the other passengers to come on board with great anticipation. Everybody was seated, and then the flight attendant gave safety instructions just in case of an emergency. Then I felt the plane slowly moving down the runway. For anyone who is experiencing this for the first time, it is the most incredible adrenaline rush one can experience without drugs. All of a sudden you are in the air and the clouds. The first time is something that you never forget.

There I was, enjoying the view on my way to Pittsburgh, Pennsylvania, for a short layover before I reached my destination, Canton, Ohio. . The plane landed in Pennsylvania, and they helped me off the plane. I was waiting and looking at all different types of people from all over the world—coming and going to another city, waiting to board another plane. I enjoyed my time just being able to travel, and my leave was not even approved yet. All that I was thinking was that this does not happen every day. I was about to board a plane one more time, which turned out to be a short ride.

I arrived at my destination safely, so from there I waited as the passengers began moving toward the front of the plane, telling the flight attendant to have a nice day. Before I knew it, the plane was empty, and all eyes were on me. I began to move forward, and then I heard, "Take your time—there is no rush." Right beside me was one flight attendant, and another was in front of me, escorting me to the front of the plane. As I looked to my left out of the window, another person was coming with a wheelchair. They took me to the luggage section, and there she was, standing with my luggage in her hand.

I had already seen her in a picture that she had sent me, so I had some idea of what she looked like, and I was not disappointed. As a matter of fact, the young man that was escorting me commented that it was nice of me to come from Baltimore, Maryland, to see my sister. He looked at my ticket. What he was saying in his mind was, "How did a man with his condition pull someone as fine as her?" My response was, "Man, do you think that I would travel all this way to see someone with an ass and hips like that for nothing? Oh, by the way, she is not my sister." Then he said, "Show you right." What he did not know was that I come from a long line of beautiful women. Then she said, "I know you guys are staring at my butt."

That was a wonderful weekend—a new city and new people. That weekend I had time to think about my future. We had breakfast and talked for hours, which was a plus for me. That weekend went by so fast, and before I knew it, it was time for me to return home. I made a phone call to my mother to see if she could pick me up at the airport on Sunday evening. Of course, she was surprised and asked, "Where are you again?" I told her where I was and what time the plane was going to be landing.

You see, my mother was concerned about me dealing with two women. One woman knew everything that I was going through, and the other one did not. My mom said, "Look here; I do not know the mess you are in." Of course, when Mom speaks, you listen.

They dropped me off, and I put my key in the door. It was business as usual. It did not seem like I was even missed. There were a few pleasantries, and that was it. After that I knew that I was in this relationship well past its expiry. You see, I had already given up my apartment that I'd had for seventeen years to be with this woman. I just wanted someone to have a dream of wanting something better in life.

She unpacked my suitcase, and that was when she asked where the rest of my silk shirts were. I told her that I had lost them in a card game, but I did win a pinky ring. She did not even put up a fuss. From that day forth, I made a vow to myself that I would never deal with two women at the same time ever again. I saw what it did to the women in my own family, and I knew that this was not for me. I stand by this to this day.

I started getting myself ready for work the next day. You see, the women that I was with did not respect me as a man. Monday could not come fast enough. We continued to talk. Who would have thought that the only way one could find peace was to go to work? In my mind, I knew that everything was about to come to an end without any healing involved.

I left her and went right into the arms of another woman. I left my job and all my material possessions and moved back with my mother for a few weeks. I received a phone call from the other woman to come back for good, and that was what I did, still searching for love and hoping that my life would be different this time. After all, I had a year's worth of leave of absence just in case this did not work out for me. Do not take my intentions the wrong way—this young lady treated me well and took care of me. But what it always came down to was having my own family and taking on the role as the man in the relationship. This never happened.

I would go looking for jobs like at Walmart and McDonald's. I remember doing my interview with McDonald's. The lady said,

"Why in the hell did you come to this town? I see from your application that you are not from here. There are no jobs in this town." To this, I said, "That has nothing to do with the interview." I knew that the interview was over. Then there was Walmart, twice. A brand-new Walmart was about to open to the public, so I just knew that I was going to get a job. After all, I had customer-service skills from my previous job. The doors opened at 7:00 a.m. for interviews, and I was the first in line. The interviewer looked over my application, and then he said the words I was dreading after seeing his face drop. "I am sorry, there are no positions available at this time." I left there absolutely crushed, thinking to myself, "That is a brand-new building. Come on, man, are you kidding me? I just want to work."

After processing that disappointment, I decided to go back on social security. I had no choice, and it took me years to get off it. In my mind, that was going backward, but I needed some kind of income coming in. I kept pushing. By this time, I had already been there for two years, and the winter was settling in, and a family friend said that the post office was hiring for the Christmas season.

Once more I went for it, and before I knew it, I was in the post office sorting mail for the season. I enjoyed every minute of my time there, which did not last long. When that was over, another change came around. This time it was Walmart again, but with a twist. I sold myself on the phone, and after talking for over twenty minutes, she asked me how fast I could get there. I told her that I was on my way. I rushed to get there, and as I began walking toward the back of the building, a gentleman began walking toward me. He looked at me and then said, "Man, they hire anybody," and started laughing.

I had to stay focused on the task at hand. All that I could think of was my goal of finalizing the deal. After all, I was thinking they must have wanted me. Who gets two interviews in one day? By this time, I was pumped up. As I opened the door, there she was. What happened next, I was not ready for. She looked at me, and she started gasping for air, like she had seen a ghost. Immediately

I knew what it was. She was expecting someone different, but she knew that she just could not say anything to me because she told me over the phone that I was hired. I could already tell that her enthusiasm had changed, but she continued with the interview, and then she said those famous words, "When something becomes available, I will give you a call. Have a nice day." We both knew that that was not true. I found myself wondering what it would take to get a job in this town. All of this happened in 2004. All I knew was that I should do everything that I could to get my job back.

I called the human resources from my previous job to inform them that I was ready to return to my old position. I did everything right according to the rules and regulations of the state of Maryland, so I assumed that everything would be fine. That was my first mistake. I did not keep my original copy of the rules and regulations; therefore, I had nothing to stand on, even though I had been approved for the leave for a year. I reached out to my union for help and explained my situation to no avail. "Do you mean to tell me that I paid dues for four years and you guys cannot help me?" I was livid. I did not know who signed off on my leave of absence or if I was terminated, so from there I decided to move to Florida with my brother. This was something that he had always wanted.

I packed up all my belongings and moved to Florida. I just knew that my brother would help me find a job—he knew a lot of people, after all. Of course, the first place we went to find me a job was Walmart. We all knew how that worked out, so after thirty days I found myself back where I had started.

I began to lose hope, and then I started to get depressed, so I began to cry out to the Lord, saying, "What have I done, Lord? Please help me!" I started reading and praising the Lord with everything in me, and the Lord did not answer me right away. He had to remove one thing out of me, and the closer that you draw to the Lord, the more you start feeling convicted. I was a mess. I kept pressing forward in my mind because, at this point, I could have easily folded and called it quits.

I had this wonderful woman from Ohio in front of me whom I respected, but she did not want to follow my lead. I understood how she felt, and we came to a mutual decision to just be friends until I got myself together. She saw how I was becoming frustrated, so I informed her family members about the decision that we had made. When the Lord is dealing with you, especially when you are living in sin, it is not a comfortable feeling. By this time, I did not care what anyone thought. Every door in front of me was shut. You see, it was not that God did not love me; he hated the sin. What I can say is this: the woman that I was with could have said, "Oh, OK then. Since you're going toward the Lord, you get the hell out of my house." She did not, because I told her that I did not want anything to do with religion. How many of you know that the Lord hates religion too? That is why I have so much respect for her. Going from her lover to her roommate was not easy without any drugs or alcohol and no job, just a monthly check. I was in my early forties, and people with disabilities do not get jobs every day.

After a few years, she began to talk to other men online, which was her right, and a relationship started. One morning after she checked her emails, I asked her if she could make up a profile for me on a Christian website. She said sure and told me to tell them the truth about our living arrangement and also to tell them that I was disabled, because I did not want any surprises from anyone if we decided to meet.

We found "Black Christian People Meet," a Christian website. The next day we were sitting in front of her computer checking her emails from the previous night. When she was done, I asked her if she would check mine. To our surprise, I had forty-something responses from around the world, from Atlanta, Georgia, to Africa—hits from everywhere. Ladies wanted to know about me, and we both began to talk to other people online. We talked about some of the women that I might be interested in, and she talked with some of them as well.

All of this was happening in the fourth year of our relationship. There was one lady who wanted me to move back to Baltimore so I would be closer to her, and of course, there were some women who were skeptical about my living arrangements. Some would say things along the lines of "You have got to be sleeping with her." We were not. When a woman shuts it off, it is over. So after dealing with all types of women, just conversing, I began to get tired.

One night I happened to be online when a young lady from the same town in which I was in said hello. I thought this was strange because no one seemed to be interested in talking with me in this town. We formally introduced ourselves, briefly talked, and that was it. I thought nothing of it. I needed a break from being online, so that was that.

By this time I was ready to go back home to Maryland. Three years had already passed. One day we were driving past Mercy Medical Hospital, and without thinking about it, I simply stated that I was going to get a job at this hospital. Weeks later I went to the volunteer department and filled out an application. Two weeks after that, they called me for an interview, which went well. Before I knew it, I was a receptionist with two other people in the cancer unit.

I enjoyed being around the people, but I still had my eye on the listing for jobs in Baltimore. After volunteering for a month or so, I got a change. I had an interview for office clerk for the state penitentiary, which did not go well. I flew back to Baltimore, and as soon as I stepped off the plane, my cell phone rang. It was Mercy Medical wanting to know if I wanted a job as an escort attendant. I said that I just landed at Baltimore Washington International Airport and that I would be back in a couple of days. The lady over the phone told me that everybody in the hospital was talking about me. I asked her if she could hold the position for me until I got back. She said she could not, that she was sorry, and they were hoping that I could come in the next day. That was the second time in my life that I had spoken something and it had manifested right before my very eyes (Rom. 4:17). This time I did not get discouraged. I flew back to Ohio with some hope, even though nothing had changed and my life was still at a standstill.

After playing some Madden, which is a great stress reliever, I decided to go back online one more time. To my surprise, there she was again. We said hello, and we said a few words. I told her that I was about to shut everything down and go back home. After talking to several women, I told this young lady that she had five minutes to call me and gave her my phone number. She called me immediately, and we began to communicate every day after that. Of course, there was no need for me to be on the website anymore, but she also had doubts about my living arrangement. To ease her fears, I set up a time when the two women could talk with one another. It went well, but she wanted to make sure that her decision would be the right one. Let me say that, as a man, you cannot fix the situation, even if you think that you can.

We continued to talk, and we began to get closer. One day the women met, the one I shared a home with and the one I was dating. The latter came over to the house to see for herself. They talked, and everything went fine, and then she left.

One Saturday afternoon I received a call from the woman I was dating asking if I could meet her for lunch. I asked my roommate if she could take me to Bob Evans, to which she said yes, so off we went. I got there a little early, so I went in and asked to be seated near a window. I told the waitress that I was waiting for a guest. She said, "All right, I'll be right back." A few minutes later, she showed up. We greeted each other, then she sat down, and we ordered our food.

After that, we talked from 4:00 p.m. to 10:15 p.m. We had to end the evening because she had to go to work the next morning. That was our first date.

Weeks went by, and everything was going well until I was asked by my new girlfriend if I would like to come over for the weekend. Of course, I said yes. We were talking every day, and we both wanted each other. It was Super Bowl Sunday, 2006. We had an enjoyable weekend without any interruptions.

By this time I began to see how beautiful she was—her smell, her walk, her hair. She just exuded so much confidence that at times, when she walked into the room, she would take my breath away. To me, she had the total package. She had everything that I had ever wanted, so after that weekend was over, my roommate told me to come and get my stuff. I was in shock and wondering what was going on. We went to where I was living, and my new girlfriend was saying, "I knew it, something was going on." I tried to convince her that nothing was going on, but she was not trying to hear me.

We pulled up to the house and my suitcase was on the front porch. I went into the house, and my roommate and I had words while my lady was waiting in the car to see what I was going to do. Of course, nothing turned out well for me at that time. While I was trying to straighten things out with my roommate, my cell phone rang. It was my new girlfriend, asking what was taking me so long, asking to talk to my roommate. In all actuality, things just kept getting worse. I decided to just leave. There I was, starting over again in my midforties, hoping that things would change, and they did.

I was with this beautiful woman, whom I had met on a Christian website. She was standing in front of me, saying that I could not live with her unless we were married. My response was something along the lines of "Who in the hell are you talking to? We barely know each other!" However, she was right. After three months of getting to know each other's ways, we were about to say, "I do." Before I knew it, we were married in March of 2007.

Starting a new life, I wanted to be the best husband I could be, but first I had to find a job. That is exactly what I sat out to do. I just wanted to do my part, so when I found out that there was a job fair in town for a potato chip company by the name of Shearer's Foods, I put in a request for a ride with Proline. Proline is a transportation service that the elderly and the disabled use. I walked in to the job fair and filled out an application. From there, I sat and diligently waited for an interview. They finally said I was next, so I sat in front.

Two young ladies who were representing the company said, "We want to hire the disabled, and we are trying to get a bus to come into this area but have not done so yet, so if you can work out your own transportation, give us a call back."

I went outside to wait for my return ride. After waiting for a while, the bus pulled up. I stepped on, and the driver and I began to talk about the interview that I'd just had. I told him they could not hire me because of my transportation problems, and then he told me, "That does not apply to you. We are curb to curb. This is not public transportation."

I called human resources right away and introduced myself. I told her what the driver told me. Then she asked me when I could return, and without thinking, I immediately said I could return tomorrow. After being evaluated, I was hired weeks later as a packer/picker. Who would have thought that I would find a job and get married in the same year? Some people may look at those two events as small things, but in my world, they are major accomplishments. I had a sense of purpose moving forward.

I still had another goal I wanted to achieve: driving. I had left my car in Maryland when I moved. I had to start again. The one problem that I was faced with was that I needed a set of hand controls, which meant that I had to be evaluated all over again. I made an appointment with the Department of Vocational Rehabilitation. You see, I had to show reason as to why I wanted to drive, because they already knew that there were other forms of transportation I could use. My pitch was that if I had my own transportation, it would make me more independent. We sat down and began to discuss my situation.

They wanted to know if I had a driver's license, and if I had a car, it would have to be fully insured. My answer to their questions was yes. One thing that I do remember was that, as we continued to talk, I was asked what my wife had to say about this. I told them that my wife did not run my house. She supported me in everything I did. They did not think I could come prepared until they began to see that I was ready for my next assignment, which was taking more driving lessons and being more independent. With that being said, I left there and waited to hear what was going to happen next.

After a few weeks, I received a call from a wonderful lady who worked in the vocational rehabilitation department's school for driving to see if we could meet to evaluate me. Of course, I said yes and asked when and where. She asked me what my work schedule looked like and where I was working. Every single one of my coworkers was happy for me. Some of them watched me drive off for the first time.

Words could not fully express my feelings for all the wonderful people who played a significant role in my life. Mrs. Lewis, who was my first landlord, did not want me to leave before my time. I have never met a landlord like her before in my life; she was hurt when I left. She was instrumental in my purchasing my first car. She introduced me to Mr. Kolege from Auto Ford Nation, who has sold me two vehicles over twenty years. We are still friends to this very day. He always gives it to me straight. I have a lot of respect for him. Just like my driving instructor, Mrs. Julie wanted me to succeed, and I did. To me, she was the best at what she did. She is a dear friend. I assume that you have already figured out that we finished what we started. I truly believe that the Lord brought those people into my life at this time.

Suddenly, everything began to change for me. I take full responsibility for my part in the failure of my marriage. What I mean is, it was my fault for letting outside forces in when I was having problems. They just made things worse. What I was accused of was adultery, which was not true. That was her way out. The truth of the matter was that she could not deal with my disability anymore. Just because I did not say anything does not mean I was not watching or listening. With that said, let me ask you this: If the tables were turned, how would you deal with being married to someone with a disability? It is no different from a spouse who is terminally ill. Would you leave?

I gave her eleven years of my life, so I am not here to put her down. If I ever speak to her again, I would thank her for the good times and the bad, but most of all I would thank her for something she said that I will never forget. We were reading the Bible and discussing what we had just read when she got up and approached me, then leaned over and looked into my eyes. She said, "I see greatness in you, but you don't know it yet." She sealed those beautiful words with a kiss and then walked away. You see, that is why I loved her. She did what a lot of women would not have done. Some just wanted to take something from me or were ashamed of me, so again I thank her, and I hope she finds what she so richly deserves.

I had to deal with a broken heart after my divorce, so I put all that I had into the Lord and my job. That is when things started to change again. One morning when I woke up, I noticed that my right knee had turned completely inward. I tried to deal with it the best way I knew, but after a week of trying to deal with my balance, it began to throw me off. Occasionally I would fall. I knew that I had to do something, so I had no choice but to begin to walk with a cane. All I did every day was go to work, come home, read, pray, and talk to the Lord. I could not afford cable, so every night I would come home and watch the biblical movies that I had on DVD until I fell asleep.

My budget was tight. I was barely keeping my head above water, and I was working forty hours a week. It just was not enough. I would come home and eat, talk to the Lord, and go to church on Saturdays when I felt led to. I was trying to put on a good front while, behind the scenes, my world was falling apart. I began to praise and worship the Lord while I was at work and home.

Then things started changing again. Only once had I experienced God's glory on this level before. I am not going to lie—I was getting desperate. What I mean is that I needed God to show up, because at this time my hours were being cut back. The company I was with was going in another direction, which was something that I did not need at this time. Sometimes I would come home at night, and there would be nothing to eat. I was falling behind on my rent. I tried to be strong; only a few people around me knew what I was going through.

What I could not believe was that this was happening to me. Friends and neighbors were giving me food. I remember calling my father and telling him that I needed food. He said, "OK, I'll mail you fifty dollars right away." I did not like asking anybody for anything, but my dad already knew that if I had to ask for something, it was serious. My brother was helping me for a while too. This was a very hard time in my life, and before I knew it, I was facing eviction and about to lose my job at the same time. How much can a man take before he breaks?

I continued doing what I knew to do, which was to keep on praising the Lord, in opposition to what I was facing. Let me tell you, it was not easy. I reached out to all the organizations that I could think of for help. To my surprise, some of the questions that were asked of me were as if I had done something wrong, like "Why did you wait so long before you asked for help?" or "There is no more funding available."

After I had explained my situation, the bottom line as to why I waited so long was that I was just trying to avoid the inevitable. This was all happening around 2019.

I came home from work one day, and on my front door was an eviction notice. One was inside my mailbox as well. I kept seeking the Lord, even though the pain that I was feeling inside was immense. I started getting numb, but I had to keep it moving.

I ended up going to eviction court, and again, the Lord showed me favor. No one showed up from the property management team, so when my name was called, the judge waited for a few minutes just to see if anyone would show up. No one did, so the judge said, "Case dismissed."

I shouted, "Praise the Lord!" The judge then asked me if I had a place to stay, to which I confirmed that I did. I left there feeling good. After losing my car and eventually getting terminated all in the same time frame, I finally felt relief. That is when I started enjoying intimacy with the Holy Ghost. He let me know that he was letting me see into the spirit realm.

THE SPIRIT REALM

Let me begin by saying I did not know what this was until I got older and started to mature as a man. Like I said before, as a little boy I could sense things around me, especially at night. The Bible calls this the gift of discernment (or a seer), and the old folks used to say that I'd had a premonition, so I began reading a book called *The School of the Seers* by Jonathan Welton. I bought every book by Mary K. Baxter and one that I had not read yet by Bill Wiese called *23 Minutes in Hell*. If you want to get closer to the Lord, this is just a start. Back in 2003, I began praising the Lord all night long while working, just to pass the time away.

One morning around 4:00 a.m., I was allowed to see into the spirit realm for the first time. This night I will never forget for as long as I live. I was a sorter and packer for a potato chip plant. It was my job to get all the bad chips before they were going to be packaged. Suddenly, the wall opened, and there I was, sitting in the chair in my living room. I got up, walked to the front door, and began running toward the rental office screaming, saying, "Come out! Come see what the Lord has done!" One of my coworkers tapped me on the shoulder, asking me if I was all right. I said yeah and asked her why. She said that she had been watching me and that I was shaking. She said it was time to go to lunch, and then I asked what time it was. She said that it was five past four. All of this happened in five minutes.

I was undone after that, so I began walking down the ramp to the lunchroom full of excitement, wanting to tell someone about what just happened. I walked by a brother on the floor, packing, who knew the Lord, so we spoke to each other. I began to tell him what just happened. Then he started laughing. He began to tell me what I just experienced was a nighttime vision. Can you imagine what the rest of my night was like? I still had four hours to go before my shift would end. I was so pumped up, and I still had to work.

I got home from work and called my wife, at the time on her job, like I did every morning, to tell her what had happened. She could tell that something had taken place, because as I was trying to explain to her what happened, my voice began to quiver as if it were happening all over again. Her response was, "Honey I'm glad for you, but I'm at work. We will talk about this when I get off from work." This never happened. All I can say to that is please support each other in the body of Christ. I say that because it is not about you anymore—Christ sees you as one. Even if you do not understand, believe it or not, the spirit realm is just as real as the natural realm. God made the spirit realm first because he is spirit (John 4:24).

With that said, let us move on. You may or may not believe what I have seen. For example, I have seen flaming eyes coming out of the wall, staring right at me while my boy CJ was with me. We were just coming from an evening of eating out, like we always did, and I saw it again. I said, "Hey, man, do you see what I see?" and he replied, "No, man, move. I have to go to the bathroom." That told me that what the Lord shows you is only for you, even if there are people around you. Also let me say, this gift was given to me because I was hungry for God.

This was not the last time this happened to me. It happens periodically, but you have to find balance to keep you sane. This is what I do: I watch lots of sports or a good movie. Somebody is always calling me about their problems. Sometimes I will take a much-needed ride, which also keeps me grounded. When the Lord says that he will inhabit the praises of his people, he means it (Ps. 22:3).

Trust me when I tell you this: when he shows up, it is the most wonderful thing one can experience. That comes by fasting, reading his word, praying, and meditating on him during your day. What I mean is he talks to me like you would, as if you were talking to a real person. Do not be surprised that the Holy Ghost answers when you have a question. I cannot begin to talk about my dreams. As I get older, my dreams are like going to the movies. That is the best way I can describe my experiences.

I was still faced with needing a place to lay my head, but the Lord was moving behind the scenes. My faith was being tested—one thing right after the other was happening. I just wanted this to stop. What I learned from all of this is that the Lord will send people into your life to bless you. He will also send people into your life to show you miracles, and a miracle is what I needed at that time.

Before I knew it, God started sending people into my life. I did not even know at the time that they provided me with everything that I needed. I did not know how this would turn out for me. When the Lord says he will never leave you or forsake you, he means it (Deut. 31:8). Until the Bible becomes alive to you through faith, you can never experience the true manifestation of his word.

All of this happened in the middle of the pandemic. I remember being at the factory, singing to the Lord again, when I heard the Holy Ghost speak to my spirit, saying, "I want you to write books." When the Holy Ghost speaks, he gets your undivided attention. I began to lift my head and look down the hall of the warehouse, and I began to hear and see people that I did not know. It was like the Holy Ghost was downloading the names of the books.

People were talking at the same time the Holy Ghost was speaking to me, and all that I could do was say to one of my coworkers, "Hey, please bring me a piece of paper and a pen quickly!" She looked confused and asked what was wrong, and I said, "Look up the hall! Don't you see that?" To this, she said, "See what, D? There is nothing there but stacks of boxes." She walked away after she said this. I was at the end of the line, folding trays to be put on the line, and at the same time the Holy Ghost was speaking. He is so amazing. In the earthly realm, things had not changed for me yet, but God was still moving on my behalf.

Eventually I did get a place again, and I was let go from my job. When I reflect on everything that happened, I believe the Lord allowed it to happen so that I would be protected, because the pandemic changed things for a lot of people. God can use unusual circumstances to bring forth his purpose. After all, He knows the beginning from the end, even when we do not understand why. I was in the same situation again, trying to deal with this thing called life. What I mean is, when you start to get older, life seems to get harder, especially when you are dealing with physical challenges every day.

Nothing but his grace and his discernment have kept me alive. These are what we all need to have a productive life. It is hard for any man to have dreams when everything around him seems to be getting worse. You see, when a man stops dreaming, he is already dead. All I ever wanted was to have a life that was as normal as possible, and now that has changed. For me to be healed would be wonderful right now, so I am going after God's glory. Shouldn't we all be going after the same thing? Did you ever take the time to think about the Scripture? When God said, "Let's make man in our image," What was he saying?

You see, every one of God's beings is good. What he has wanted then and what he wants now are the same—a relationship with his creation. Just imagine having all this love within you and having no one to share it with after speaking things into existence. You see, it was God, the angels, his creation, and then man. Before man, all of God's creations worshipped him and adored him, and he was pleased with what he had made. He is not done until you realize how much he loves you as well. You will never experience his true love; that is why it is important to mention Adam and his role in shaping mankind's relationship with God. You see, Adam came out of God first because God is light, and then God's mist hovered over the face of the Earth. God formed him from the dust of the ground, then Jehovah God breathed life into Adam, and Adam became a living soul. That is when the covenant was made between God and man (Gen. 2–7).

When Adam first saw God, he looked just like him. The same glory that God had, Adam had on him as well. There is no limit to man when you have God's glory on you. Adam's intellect had to have been great because he named all the animals. Albert Einstein only used 25 percent of his brain, and he could not touch Adam or King Solomon, all because of the glory of God on these men. Ever since then, man has always craved God's glory. Who is to say that if man had not sinned, how smart would he have been? Only God knows, you see. Even the angels were intrigued with Adam because they had never seen a human. Do not forget the angels that are flying over God's head nonstop, saying, "Holy, holy, holy is the Lord God all mighty who was, who is, and who is to come." Every time that they look at the throne, even they are in awe, because they see something different every time too (Rev. 4:8).

Then God created Adam with free will. I often wonder if there was ever a time when they all were together, just standing there looking at one another; quadruplets—the father, the son, the Holy Ghost, and Adam. That is just the way I think. That is why I find the spirit realm so fascinating. This did not happen to me overnight; it was years in the making. Every man who had an encounter with the Lord had a life-changing experience. I love to hear other people's stories because that gives me hope.

Would you believe there are some Christians who are losing hope because they need a touch from God and have been waiting, just like me, for a long time? Please never give up, and do not let your feelings get in the way. This is why I am expecting his glory to show up in the natural. You see, from the beginning of creation, Adam had God's glory on him. This means Adam was red clay, or the son of red earth from the Hebrew text; that glory was shining through his very being while he was walking in the garden, and all creation saw it on him. It was coming out of him like a red light; this was the blood covenant between God and Adam. This was how they could communicate with one another—because of the glory. Without the glory, even Adam would not have been able to go into the presence of God until things changed. It was never God's intention for man to experience good and evil; in Genesis 3:6–10, the words that one could use are disobedience and shame of what they lost.

The Lord checked Adam first by saying, "Who told you that you were naked?" That is when Adam realized that the glory of God was not on him like it was before; if that was not true, Adam would have never covered himself up. He lost communication with God because sin separates us from God. His free will was not taken from him or his learning capability, which had to have been off the charts. Think about every animal on the face of the Earth—a lot was going on at that time. Do you ever wonder what God had in store for mankind before the fall? I believe that we will one day know all the answers to all of God's goodness for mankind, and this is why I love the spirit realm. When God shows up, things change in the natural realm, which makes you draw closer to God. You see, when we all get to Heaven, it is going to be a busy place, talking with loved ones and the people who you read about in the Bible standing right in front of you. Greatest of all, Jesus Christ, our Lord the father God, and the Holy Ghost.

No more pain or death. Old things make way for everything new, like God's throne and the living creatures. Just imagine that the Lord will allow you to see these things while you are on the Earth, just like John and Ezekiel saw these things. Even though they were chosen, they still were men. The Bible is so real. With all the experiences that I have been through in my life, there is no comparison to the things of God. You do not forget them, so the question is, how close do you want to know him? Or rather, can we get to a place where we are just like Adam was with God?

WHAT'S IN YOUR MOUTH?

Let me be the first to say, always be mindful of what you say to people, even if you do not care for that person. I know it is hard at times, but when you hurt someone with harsh words, you cannot take those words back. It is all about controlling one's temper, and I am guilty of this as well. The tongue no man can tame (James 3:8). That is why I should not be surprised when Christians are offending one another with words. You would not believe what I have been called by people in the body of Christ, just because I did not do what they said or do what they thought I should have done, or that I simply disagreed with them. The words are too shocking to even put on paper. I expect that from nonbelievers, but not Christians.

What I have learned is that I have to love you, but I do not have to like your behavior. What I have heard with my ears is that one's gift has nothing to do with one's character. When your gift is not in operation, you will see a person's flaws. I know that the Lord will forgive you for how you mistreat people, if you belong to him. I also believe there are consequences to one's actions—what I mean is that you are going to reap what you sow. The price is too high. The one thing that mankind thinks that we have is time, and in all actuality, we do not. Do not mistreat people because you know that you can.

My life means something. If that were not so, the Lord would not have allowed me to be born. I cannot help the way I came into this world. All the other people who were born with some type of physical or mental deformity will not be forgotten. Trust me when I say that God sees you, and he loves you when nobody else does. Always remember that he gave his life for you, even when times get hard and the storms come and you ask yourself why. You see, I do not believe the old folks when they say, "What does not kill you makes you stronger." The truth of the matter is that God showed you his mercy, and he gave his angels charge over you. So if you are not going to do good by us, please leave us the hell alone. We already have enough that we have to contend with daily.

Love—what is love, or how does one define love? It is a four-letter word; that is, we loosely love without action. It is just a four-letter word. I am not saying that everyone that I have met in my lifetime was bad, but I would like to know what draws you to me. Is it curiosity? Is it the Holy Spirit? Do you feel sorry for me? Or do you just want to say hello? With that being said, I want to thank all the people who just want to say hello. I appreciate you so much.

Ask yourself why you do not see a lot of disabled people with normal people. Let us talk about it. Why is that? When we do, why is it so inspiring to others? It took me half of my life to realize that there was greatness inside of me. All my adult life, all I ever heard was that I had some of it but not enough, as far as intelligence goes. That bothered me for years. Then God placed a physical itching inside of me that just recently went away. Now I am doing what he asks me to do, no matter what the people say or do. They say to themselves that they are trying to help you, but they are hating on you because they cannot believe what you are doing. They are waiting for your blessing.

IN THE WILDERNESS

Let me be the first to say that this is a place where one does not want to enter too many times in one's life. Unfortunately I have been there more than once. It is a place that will make you or break you. There are so many trees and narrow walking spaces. Needless to say, there is one way in and one way out. The question remains: What is one going to do while he or she is trying to find the answers as to why they kept ending up here? Is it because you did not heed the warnings, because you think that you are in control? Do you remember the last time that you were here? A young puppy was turning around and around chasing its tail, but he never looked at you until it was time for you to leave. He was trying to tell you, please come back, and if you do, I will be here when you come back. You cry out to the Lord to set you free. Meanwhile you should be looking at what is going on around you, so that you will not repeat the same mistakes over and over again. Let us take a closer look at why you are in the same predicament again. The puppy symbolizes one's immaturity—you cannot see what is around you with your spiritual eyes. Or is your flesh involved as well? Also, you are protecting that which is around you; that is, your guardian angel who has been with you since the day you were born. You see, every bad decision that we make does not come from God. Sometimes you have to go through the wilderness to reach your destination. Today I say, Holy Spirit, please help with all pieces of the fruit of the spirit, which is patience, before I make any decision, because my life matters.

THE JOURNEY: WHEN IT SEEMS LIKE IT'S OVER, IT'S OVER

I would like to take time to thank my best friend, the Holy Spirit. When I was close to death, you were always there for me. Thank you so much. You never gave up on me, even when I could not take it anymore and I wanted to come home because life was beating me up. Now I know why. The days and nights when you did not say anything, it was for a reason. Even if I could not hear you, you were always with me. I would like to say that I am sorry for not acknowledging you enough. I am eternally grateful for what you do in my life. Amazingly, we as a people have so many trials and tribulations before we wake up and realize that we can make a difference. I hope that everyone who does not fit in according to society's standards never gives up on God, because he has a plan for their life. Just be ready when he speaks.

HOLDING ON TO HIS MIGHTY HAND

God began to speak to me at the end of 2020 until this very day, through his word and through my spirit. It is as if someone else is giving you instructions as to what to do next. It is the coolest thing one can ever experience. The mere fact that the God of the universe takes the time and cares about what is in your future is mind-boggling to me. If you had asked me just three years ago if I would be writing a book, I would have told you no way. First of all, I did not know that I had it in me to write. It is therapeutic, funny, and emotional all at the same time. If I would you tell all the things that people have done to me, then this would be a tell-all book. This is what I needed in my life at the time. Even though this was years in the making, I am so grateful that the Lord chose me to do this assignment and that I was allowed to share some of my experiences with those who think their lives have no meaning every day.

It has been hard for me to have to deal with the physical challenges of life—trust me when I say there are times when I get tired—but if my self-affirmation can inspire someone else to never give up, then my life is not in vain. With that being said, I hope that the Lord touches you as he has touched me. Until we meet again, God bless all of you.

As for me, the Bible has to become alive in my life; if not, it is just words. But until one experiences the supernatural thing of God, ask yourself, Do you know him? It has been my experience that you have to have both for balance and for spiritual growth.

As I was saying, on January 22, 2024, around five, I was beginning to start my day after stepping out of the shower. I looked into the mirror. I didn't want to believe what I thought I saw, so I looked again, but in my mind I was thinking to myself, "Did I have a stroke in my sleep?" So that's when I called my counselor and asked her if she could step away for a moment. Without hesitation, she said, "I'll be right there." She could sense that something was wrong.

So I opened the door, and she walked in. Then I asked her to turn on the light, and did she notice anything about my face? That's when she said, "Yes, you need to go to the emergency room." You see, I was still trying to deal with the initial shock of what was happening to me. That's when I started calling everybody that I could think of. Some wouldn't answer, and some did because it was eight in the morning. Why do we think, when an emergency occurs, everybody that you know will respond to your need right away? And when they don't, you start becoming angry because of your own fear. So I had to calm down inside, and before you knew it, I was on my way to the emergency room, which took five minutes to get to.

So there I was, being put into a wheelchair, waiting to be seen, and still trying to think of what had happened. Up to the window I go. I began to explain my situation. She handed me a clipboard and said to fill out the form, and do you have insurance? After giving the receptionist my paper work, she said, "Someone will see you shortly."

So after waiting for ten minutes, the side door flew open, and they called my name. I rushed into the back. All that I could remember them saying was, "They are probably going to keep you if you had a stroke." So there I was, in a room, and the nurse was saying, "Take off all your clothes and put on this robe." As they helped me on the examining table, one by one here they came, saying, "We want to check your vital signs and do a CAT scan. And we need urine from you as well." This took all day. The nursing staff were coming in and out all morning. We were waiting for the doctor to say what the results of the tests were and to be examined by him. Hours passed. Then the doctor came in and introduced himself, leaned over, and said, "It looks like you may have Bell's palsy, but we want to make sure that you didn't have a stroke."

So there we were, waiting for the results from the test. Two more hours had gone by, and the shift had changed. So about something to four, the doctor came in again and said what he had already suspected: "You have Bell's palsy. Everything else came back fine. I'm going to give you two prescriptions, and I want you to make an appointment with your primary care doctor." I remember him saying, "We see this all the time," like it was supposed to be normal. That's what was going on in my mind. I was still dealing with the initial shock.

After coming home and settling down, there I was alone again with my thoughts, and this is what I said to myself: "Two palsies. Wow, do you not think one is enough?

So without the Holy Spirit, I could not survive this walk called life. You see, I take everything to him. I am so glad that he is there. I talk to a man that I can't see, but I can hear him at times. He lives inside of me, and these are some of the things I talk to him about: Why did you bring me here like this? And when am I going to be healed? And why is life so hard for us because we are different? I know that you care, and I know that every question you will answer one day with all due respect. Let us talk about it.

ABOUT THE AUTHOR

Darrell Mills, a Baltimore native, relocated to Canton, Ohio in 2002. Inspired by his faith and a desire to uplift those with disabilities, Mills penned *The Forgotten People*. His writing serves as a powerful reminder that everyone's life has purpose and significance. Mills' passion extends beyond his writing, as he actively strives to raise awareness about the importance of recognizing and valuing all individuals. Guided by divine inspiration, his work enlightens readers on the inherent worth of every life, encouraging empathy and understanding. Darrell Mills, through his book, seeks to inspire and create a more compassionate world.